THE GIRL AQUARIUM

Other books by Jen Campbell

FICTION

The Beginning of the World in the Middle of the Night

CHILDREN'S BOOKS

Franklin's Flying Bookshop
Franklin and Luna Go to the Moon

POETRY

The Hungry Ghost Festival

NON-FICTION

Weird Things Customers Say in Bookshops
More Weird Things Customers Say in Bookshops
The Bookshop Book

JEN CAMPBELL

The Girl Aquarium

BLOODAXE BOOKS

ISBN: 978 1 78037 449 9

First published 2019 by
Bloodaxe Books Ltd,
Eastburn,
South Park,
Hexham,
Northumberland NE46 1BS.

www.bloodaxebooks.com
For further information about Bloodaxe titles
please visit our website and join our mailing list
or write to the above address for a catalogue

Supported using public funding by
ARTS COUNCIL
ENGLAND

Cover design: Neil Astley & Pamela Robertson-Pearce.

Digital reprint of the 2019 Bloodaxe Books edition

'I don't know how to answer. I know what I think, but words in the head are like voices underwater. They are distorted.'

JEANETTE WINTERSON, *Oranges Are Not The Only Fruit*

ACKNOWLEDGEMENTS

Poems from this collection have been published in *Agenda, Magma, The Manchester Review, The Prose Poem Project, The Rialto* and *Shearsman*. Several also appeared in my poetry pamphlet *The Hungry Ghost Festival* (The Rialto, 2012) and in the anthologies *Cast: The Poetry Business Book of New Contemporary Poets* (smith | doorstop, 2014) and *Land of Three Rivers: the poetry of North-East England* (Bloodaxe Books, 2017). These poems have placed in the Battered Moons Competition, Plough Prize, Sentinel Poetry Competition, Tongues and Grooves Competition, Wigtown Poetry Competition, and won both the Jane Martin Poetry Prize and an Eric Gregory Award.

Many thanks to Liz Berry, Melissa Lee-Houghton, Michael Mackmin, Max Porter and Christopher Reid for reading an early version of this manuscript.

I'm very grateful to the Wellcome Library for their maze of books.

Thank you, Neil Astley, for giving this collection a home.

CONTENTS

III

I

Concerning the Principles of Human Knowledge

The sky outside looks like rain
looks like the sky
looks like water.

When I try and tell my story, I take a deep breath and vomit
saplings of myself
that tell translations of the same story.

They dance dances to the music of the rain
in the sky
that looks like water.

And I try to explain that all stories can coexist and I am
many separate things
that disagree with one another
and that is ok.

Because in the forest that is many other forests, I found my lungs.

Because in the forest that is many other things, apart from other forests,
I left my camera to record the sound of the rain
falling from the sky
that looks like water.

I have that sound here.
You can listen to it.
It exists.

And if we are seventy percent water does that mean that we are
constantly falling from the sky? Towards forests that exist on paper.

If I record us, would people hear it? All our many different selves
hurtling towards the ground.

Would they think we are extraordinary, dancing in the rain?

#1

Caitlin has ghosts on her tongue, seaweed in her bladder and trees in her groin. She is Mary: growing, growing in a Victorian fruit bowl. She is a washing machine. She scrubs her moon fingers when the people sleep. Caitlin is a double-harbour. She is the base of Noah's ark and she doesn't know Noah. No to Noah and yes to beasts. Dead and alive within the branches of her and her cape and her saucepan lids. Caitlin is in a band. Caitlin *is* the band. She sings all the instruments of the voices collected in the pit of her soul. The forest is listening and the dead are here, too. No to Noah and yes to Caitlin. She waters her lips and the dead stars shine.

Girl Lunar

You run across the garden – a pair of lungs. Blue fruit
and attic-faced. Your eyes parachutes. The sky is black
and I can't make out your toes as they Morse code
the grass. *This is the night*, you say.
You say: *we are the night*. The night is humming
and it is cold. A giant, outdoor freezer and I wait
for our kiss to become kitchens. A film
where you are running and I am still.
     Fish-eyed.
I picture teeth along the cloud line.
I need you to help me, I say, panicked.
My breath is clouds.
       I need you, I say.
             Moth breath.
We are in the garden of dark matter.
Your face doubles in the pond.

The Exorcism of the North Sea

On Sundays we sing.
Ghost birds. You lead us
to the southern cliffs
with our Girl Guide tents.
The sun is ours.
We have verses to prove it,
tucked in the hems of our
midwinter pockets.
We are snow globes.
Along the rows of
whitewashed caravans
young boys peer
out and whistle if
their mums aren't home.
Everything is seen through
murky glass. The sea lurches.
Someone should save
the soul of her. Lukewarm
and watered down,
holding all the girls
in bathing suits.
We stretch out our
carol sheets
and hum like bees.

Memories of Your Sister in a Full Body Wetsuit

Letters had been found in bags. Cut and stick newspaper notes
like it's the movies. So we took her away.
She looked out of place against the motor. It was its corners
and her hair as she pushed down the back seats to sit.

Before then, when I'd seen her, she'd just been showered.
I caught her glances in vases, in newly-washed milk bottles
before you threw them on the front step.
She used to dodge under tables away from roaming eyes.

Home away from home.

We three sang along the road, fake fur across my knees.
She asked to cradle old cassette tapes. They opened
up with sound, like flannels sold in town
tossed in water till they bloomed.
That was the nineties: bulk-bought in Disney,
petals shoved into pores and us scrubbing in the bath
until all our sins were drowned. *Amen.*
You sped up then to make sure all the cruel things got left behind.

The sea was far; you could guess it by the gulls.
You took us to a lighthouse – her nose up in the air
and blue mascara in her fringe.

Her fingers waving on the glass.

You said you used to visit before your mum found amber bottles.
Before your sister's operations, for she'd arrived in this world
        swimming.
Your dad hunting for receipts.

Now, kids call your sister *selkie*, trying hard to make it stick.
Her left leg is weaker, only half the bones
and unknowns cry
she must've done a bad thing, back then, back when.
Like you can bottle karma and shower in it. *Screw it.*

So, we left a canoe strapped to the car roof, our bags full of lycra.
You blew bubbles and she grinned. Your knuckles red.

We changed our clothes in the car park
with all its people watching – their eyes tracking scars
that snaked up her legs and down again, like scissors.
Like rivers.

We put our faces through those portrait boards:
a sailor and a mermaid.

Come on, she giggled, stepping out onto the shore
like she had lived there once before
jumping into the listening sea.

You took my hand.
The water hissed around our calves.

I remembered armbands like blood pressure monitors.
The pounding in my ears.
Water shooting up my nose and the taste of anaesthetic.

Appendix

It was in the news today
about that boy who was found
inside a cow.

Curled into the tightest comma, paused:
his toes tangled with intestines and

each hand ploughed
into a separate stomach.

The pages curl under my doormat,
coated like a football of straining bladders.
All papier-mâché headlines.

Some poor boy from a nursery rhyme
trying to break free from stretching jaws.

Perhaps he thought it would be warm in there,
going straight for the milk from the inside.

Movement

On the bus home, I think of all the constellations
hiding under my skin.

I think of the word vein
and decide I don't like it.

I think of you and how – maybe
you flit and fit
within a different galaxy.

I write in my notebook in code
and think about gravity.

I think that maybe we're both lost
in the skins of human planets.

The Girl Aquarium

At half-term the aquarium is at its busiest.
They hire street vendors to come inside and hand out beer.
Candy floss for the kids whose parents don't care.
The corridors heave with barbecue.
Too damp to strike a match.

On the guided tours, there are labelled doors.
Tickets colour-coded for separate rooms.
Interactive exhibits. Gas-powered lifts.

Girls swim either side and finger the joints.
Their handprints broken like starfish.

In the feeding room: girls with extra limbs.
They scuttle into corners, pretend they're shy.
In the sun room: girls with beetle eyes.
Iris headbands blinking
at all the mobile phones.

Hashtag girls.
Hashtag half-girls.
Hashtag nothing you've ever seen before in your tiny little life.

A teenage boy bangs the window, gives them the finger.
The girls rush forward, lips open, kissing the glass.
The parents eat popcorn and miss their mouths
while their headphones chatter on about science-based things.

The girls wear numbers like netball jackets
glowing in the dark.

In the purple room: floating body parts.
When the timers hiss, these fly
to meet each other. Greet each other.

Humming choirs and muttered blues.

An intern paints this
singing underwater songs.

The tanks in the basement hold everlasting sperm.
Small bottles of it sell in the aquarium gift shop.
Mothers keep it hidden behind clocks, atop fires.
Some bury it in their garden, hoping baby plants will grow there.
A girl down the road prays her sunflowers will open to show
bright blue eyes like her grandmother had.

All the better to see you with.

Back in the central tank, pregnant women come to swim.
They meditate beneath the waves, looking through each others' skins.
The water is thick with unpleasant wishes.
Not mine. Please yours.
They sign contracts to give up their inner child, *if.*

Most visitors do not choose to see the top floor birthing pool.
Those who do bring dark glasses.
They run their hands through their growing hair
and count the strands. They place bets. Sit cross-legged
counting kidneys, hands, and teeth and toes.

There is one man, pulling ice cubes from his pockets.
This is not a competition! he shouts: *yet, life makes you a winner!*
The women groan, lash out at his heels.
Their bellies upwards towards the sky.
Like, oh – so many floating worlds.

When it comes to it, they do not look.
The successful few are praised and shunned.

The unmothers wash themselves and hurry home,
their hair still wet and bleeding.

Half-full

Girl of organs.
Girl within a wolf.
Cold fury girl.
Girl captain.
Half the sky fall girl.
Livers of a girl.
Metamorphous girl.
Girl without a room.

Girl within a crab dress.
Sidestep girl, pincered girl.
Girl underwater. Sailor girl.
Sold. Path labelled to a she girl.
Go girl. Gull girl.
A mouth of girls.

Etymology

In the garden we are surrounded by lady bugs.
Birds, Caitlin whispers. Her electric hair flying. We feel
for leaf bones. Pound our faces into liquorice soil.
No one is home and the old house is sinking.
Next door there is a man who crouches below hedges.
He watches. Through the petals
we are orange girls. Caitlin peeling her hair like fruit rind.
Some days I feel she is a hotel. She needs cleaning
from all the ghosts that continue to sleep inside of her.
She has a grass stain on her upper lip. Pickling.
These spiders are whales on stilts, she laughs.

What he did can be found in Genesis

He loved wild things because they matched how he'd fold girls' hands
against the wallpaper.

In the heat he swore blind there were lasses there.
In the hedgerow, running.
Like some theatrics he'd been dragged outside to see.
Crawling down on their hands and their knees.
Like they were praying.

Luminiferous Aether

In the cousins' room the lightbulbs crack.
There are limbs reaching out
for the Peter Pan collars of speechless girls.
They wait in skin that is not their own.
In the dark they forget the names
of each others' mothers. They kneel.
They feel the fur creep to their necks
from the blue-bitten wolves.
In fractured handbags they carry
knitted souls. They stretch themselves.
Their heels find conkers and the stumps of trees.
The stench of wheat beer breadcrumbs.
Outside there is music to cut their bones.
In groups, they search their hair for keys. Their poor
scarred heads. They know too many things now.

I wish to tell you body parts

The heart of a young girl.

The heart of a pig.

The heart of the matter.

The heart as brains.

The heart as wood.

The heart within its glossy feathers.

The heart runs.

The heart boils. The heart burns.

The heart beats underground.

The stomach of a small boy.

The stomach of a house.

The stomach of a hiding place.

The stomach of a boat.

To stomach it.

The stomach that swallows itself.

The stomach snowballs.

The stomach shines. The stomach churns.

The stomach eats the night-time sky.

The lungs of a wise woman.

The lungs of a centipede.

The lungs of dancing figurines.

The lungs of half-born seas.

The lungs as peppered earth.

The lungs as bubbled rock.

The lungs pop.

The lungs melt. The lungs yell.

The lungs bloom underwater.

The Magician's Daughter

Parched, we swim to an island that can cure us all of sleep. Who has time for dreaming when a young girl can pull a night sky from a knapsack? Endless animals tumble out of crafted darkness to the beach. It is carnage. My phone splutters, and as our blank eyes droop, the young girl tells us that we should eat the sand. We do it gladly. With glass on our lips, we applaud her father's wisdom and ignore her pleading eyes as daylight seeps out from her gums. It trickles down her front, all sunbeams and clotted rainbows. It would be rude of us to stare, so – we continue to consume the earth.

The Chicken, the Egg and My Sister

My sister didn't mind killing chickens; it was the killing
of cows that bothered her most. I caught her once, red all down
her front. It was the eggs, and the burnt soldiers.
The world is not a foetus, she would say. W*e do not need
to be children.* She'd stand on the power-washed patio stones
bleeding the hen neck into a milk pail. At night
she threw a coat over her head, carried eggs in baskets
and dragged the bucket to the slaughterhouse two miles
up the road. She drew equations down the side
with her fingertips. She threw eggs at the windows, hoping
her hatred would cook them into eyes.
She said the dead cows moaned there.

On Sundays she'd stalk supermarkets,
buy all the beef she could find and reassemble it
on the back lawn. A meat scarecrow.
She poured skimmed milk on top and watched the daisies wilt.
We ate pickled sandwiches on an old picnic mat
waiting for the flies and other animals. She listened
for any sound it made. *Do you think it lives?* she asked,
her mouth full of crumbs.

The Patron Saints of Animals

No one mentions the dead bird hanging in the hall.
Tommy takes a stick to it. Feathers fall across the rug
that our grandpa dragged over from the orchard fields.
Makes it smell of blood apples. Of carol-singing cheeks,
their glow nicked straight from the freezer.
                                        We practise singing
in the basement, cool our hands on mother's solid stock.
In the kitchen, knives are sharpened up for beef joint.
Chicken eggs in pots sit humming on the window ledge.

My task is putting prayers out on the napkins
like a specials board. I divide the words as I would cut grain.
No one crows for us in the morning; it is our job to wake ourselves.
Mother calls this time our crystal dawn –
it means she often misses breakfast.
She feeds the kid goats at the table out of bottles. Old body parts
we no longer need. Father reddens but does not speak.
Upstairs the top sow has the larger bath.

Tommy chimes out that it's one o'clock. He's found
Christmas crackers to break open on the hour. He puts
the plastic toys up on the mantel. They sit between our cloven hooves.

Father brings our biggest cow in from the outside cold.
She clatters on the table top, breaking soup bowls underneath.
I pinch my thigh, don't squeak a thing. Use a butter knife
to file my dirty nails.
Father raises his prayer crown high.
I remember days when those were pirate hats
and sometimes boats. We close our eyes and think
of animals, low bleatings sounding in our paper-wrapped throats.
Tommy's laughing at the joke he found.

Mother puts her palms on the cow's warm flank, counts upwards,
guessing meals. I think how many of us could fit inside
and be reborn with leather shoes.
There is a flutter in the hallway – grandpa's cough.
We could feed here for a long while, I think, then hang her udders up
on the chandelier. Fill them high with marzipan and dance below.
We'd be barefoot on the broken plates, singing winter songs for food.

II

Hero

noun
man of strength.
synonyms: brave, champion, man of courage,
great man, star, lion, favourite, darling.

Pull up a seat.
An uncomfortable seat.

We ask that you focus.
Please switch off your mobile phones.

In the film with the hero, the hero is beautiful.
Darling, the beautiful hero is saving the world.

In the film with the hero, the villain has scars.
The skin-mapped villain is killing for fun.

In these films with their heroes, their lions, their stars,
the world nurtures itself, darling.
The world understands blame.

'I think, you see,' the director explains.
'That there is nothing wrong...
with the body...with it being used to show...
you know?... The audience needs to know.
...We need to tell them...
This is a world where we feel at home.'

Look here, darling.
Try not to stare.

We watch.
They watch.
He, she, it watches.

Miss Eliza's Skeleton Factory

The bones: the way they bowl across the science lab and match the coats of those who hold them. The way they close in on themselves as elephant ears and paint beneath the skin. Clicking paper clips. Crushed down teeth. Airport luggage. The female bones and their tap dancing lessons. Unskinned. Raining and huddled like dominoes.

The Doll Hospital

First, they say, you must think of the shape.

Hold it.
>
> The question-marked spine.
> The colour of the eyes and if you look closely
> the fox-tongue-rabbit-heart-barely-there grin.

We each make half.   Carved.
Kneading grey the texture of calf tongue.

I lick the edges, fold an envelope ear
and listen for wings. Moth or magpie or dragonfly beats.

My mother claimed I had changeling feet
dancing in dirt water   pulling a ragged doll
through fairy rings when she summoned me home for tea.

I cup my palms.

> Little fishling.
> I wonder if we should roll her hair like starfish.
> Watch it flicker the colour of raspberry-plum.

We hum, take turns.   Pirouette
her little body so her organs align marbled planets.

   Hush.

How ridiculous that we should be allowed to craft,
and mould and hope   as we coat her in a water glaze

                    then bake.

In the dying light we rest and wait.

Up north, they say, if you cover their limbs in hospital white
you might later dig for victory.

So we pull on our shoes and step out into snow.

      It is a long road.

We bury our porcelain children in the flickering woods.
Our soiled hands   tangled in juniper roots
and you hand me a crown   fit for an unmarked country.

The Bear

I sit in the dark in a blue jumper that scratches and ask you how you would draw a bear if you'd never seen one before.

You don't seem to understand the question.

It's a very important question, I say.

It's a stupid question, you say. I know what bears look like. I'll draw one for you now.

The paper is too dark to see.

I steal your pencil and persist that you have never seen a bear in the flesh and photographs are all well and good but you have never touched a bear or hidden from a bear or felt the breath of a bear on your very human skin.

Also, how do you know I am not a bear? I ask.

Because you're not, you say. Go to sleep.

I bristle under the duvet, my hot lungs Ursa Major.

The Angel of the North

I always wondered why   a lass would stand on a hillside
with her arms spread wide   like she's reachin for the world.

But there are newspaper chiefs

what are takin her photo   with all of them chattin
like she might   have been theirs.

So I stood on a bank   tilted in me back garden
and waited impatient   for me skin to rust and fade.

And it's weird, I keep sayin – I divvent knaa if I like it
even though she's a sign what's to welcome us home.

'Cause if she cannit move, does it matter? And where are her eyes?
And if her mouth cannit open   can she still taste the snow?

What food does she eat and what language should I use?
And does she know she's a giant stretched out in the wind?

If we take it in turns   to stand facing the sky
will she know that we're there? Will she feel less alone?

Swimmin

I knew, like, that I was born different. Tall, see,
lighthouse heights. And me eyes was a warnin.
Flashin cinemas across the grasses.
Lasses, all of em, tearing flames out their bleedin hair.
Black and white sailin boats gannin away.

You came ter watch us. Flew across the puddles
with yer chest near hammerin. A lass kept
in a jam jar – only just let out.
            Alreet? Yer new words stumblin.
Yer bonny lips photographs.

There was us: two girls w'lampshade mouths.
Wor new found land.
Yer nana's patio wet beneath wor feet. Blisterin cald
and there was owls lurkin back, carryin me words.
Yer black black hair, canny like steam. Yer bird eyes, coal.
Yer body a house for us.   Its sea rooms like yem.

Birdlasses

W'get their souls.
Knock em down from downy birch.
Catch their spirits, like. Get em good.
Out comes a spirit – sprite! – dancin air. Blackbird
face out on the ground. Yella mouth.
Yellin quiet, nowt. W'net it – quick. Reet.
Tug it in.

Have yous ever seen   a birdish soul
captured tight fist   in a money box?
It shines, right   like yer skeletons.
It floats up   on all wor tongues.

A divvent knaa how w'breathe it inwards.
W'suck the life out through wor lungs.

Let it settle on wor burnin chests.
Chirrup on right   through wor shoulder blades.

Spirits pokin out through wor fingernails.

Out back, pull on bin bags fer w'feathered tails.
Shove some blackbird gloss in w'hair.

W'can flap w'selves.
Pout out wor new born beaks.

Us as birdlasses. Jumpin canny fly.
Gannin cloudwards on wor own.

Netted

And then they caught us.
Eyes shoutin like they was radio.
Me hair aal up in their fists
like a cloud. It's long now.
Down t'ma navel – cause then aal
the black is like a cave what I sit in.
What I can sing in. W'voices hidin
in aal the corners
like I'm radio, too.

And then they caught us – me 'n' Caitlin.
We was dancin our way yem.
Fairgrounds in wor eyes
blazin out like dancin lions
and me stomach a stinkin jellyfish
aal zip-zappin around.

And then they caught us
when we was whisperin.
And their fingers got me mouth.
The hiccoughs of the ocean
aal drippin down wor blouse.
And the sounds was gannin manic
like we was trapped underground.

And then they caught us.
Said we was danger.
Said our queer souls was a well –
lookin at us like w'fishes
what swam but should've drowned.
Yet, I think me soul's a lighthouse
and I cling t'Caitlin's arm.

Our voices singin
from aal the corners
like we's mermaids in the dark.

Merlasses

Down the chippy they call w'sirens. Blazin like
red fire engines the lot of us. Rucksacked tails
brushin along the backs of bus seats. Gannin to the waves.
Sometimes I swear I'm movin, but I ain't. Me dad says
I'm well-fard, and it's all a girl is good for.
Me tail's bright purple, all the sequins yammerin.
There are four of us. We do it in divers' pools,
they tret us right there. Changin after swimmin class
so as I'm half in mesel. Half out – me mouth all pouts
and glass eyeballs.
                      Swimmin yem.
The water's goose flesh against wor plastic fins.

The lads pay to watch us. Caitlin's pink and Tara's
red-burn cheeks canny near blowin. We play at drowin.
Plodge until wor lungs are blue. In stories we was
sailors' dreams. Rock-slammin and them huntin for the zip.
Now we're slot machines. Holdin wor breath.
To fit inside, we wrap wor legs tight-like with elastic bands.
Costumed. *Show us it!* they yell, banging fists.
I cannit breathe.
Me heart is pulsin, pulsin. The fish-scaled chlorine.
How much for it? They clout
their five pound notes against the glass.

Small Infinities

If there are fireflies
on the tablecloth –
if there are not. If
the mother of all
mothers has yet to
land beside the
summerhouse, and
if she never will.
If somewhere
you are curling
days around our
great syllables.
Soul-spitting if
splitting had
decided to
shorten itself.
And, if yes,
then there's that
hiss we made
against your
father's broken
caravan. And if
the light bulbs
are too bright
to hold
then we can
sew them inside
our clumsy t-shirts.
If we can lie
down on
your tablecloth –
imagine
every black hole.

If we
can become
luminescent insects.
If we
can light up
our purple sky.

A Song of Herself

Before gifts and weekend bus rides, all was forest: the hair and
the house. She hung her voice from the height of firs, and the
castle was condensation. It rained only when she prayed for rain.
Sometimes the salt air. Sometimes baskets from the wings of planes.
She slept as if still moving. The floor voices, and the she-owls.
She passed through floors using mirrors. Her lungs inverted and
grew as glass. In the basement she bred hounds for the feasting.
Gold mugs forged by those on boats. Sometimes the foundations
moved and her hair was sea. If she was sick, the empty cages
covered it. Her clothes stretched within her skin. Through the
branches she saw the women. They lined up at the traffic lights,
not knowing where they were.

Angel Metal

We stand underneath and pray to her.
We do not know why we pray. Sometimes
it's hard, the grass. It's the frost here.
You hold my hand like it's the theatre.
The applause is too low down,
winding under us like electric rabbits. You
pick my arms up and spread them out
so we are matching. Our woollen scarves
touch our noses – catch our breath
like cloth balloons. We dig our feet into the soil
and stamp down into the very deep.
Somewhere below, the river sleeps with a lady,
screeching. She has arms that could carry boulders
to the edge of cliffs. We wait for her
to throw us down. Our parents, stiff, pretend
they are not watching. They sit on sofas behind
their damning papers. We are not children.
We wait alone in the coldest times while people read.
They say we have taken something
they cannot put back inside of us. They say
we are building blocks, and purse their ragged lips.
I picture barren fields transformed into supermarkets
with bars across their naked windows.
I am warm inside. We wait.
We fill our pockets with frozen peaches.

On Crucifixion

When we throw our arms out, we billow. Near the ground, the bell boys bray. Their elephant heads and misfit trousers. With the birds burning, I long for rooms. For rocks.

My blindfolded mouth. They cannot see the half of me.

They say that if the horse's head was titled we could be violins. Melted faces merged with sky, and we would stamp the windowed spirits.

To see taste: it would be in white dresses. All the shades. My pinprick head. My flammable legs. Them, tearing at my shoes and hoping for animal noises. My senses flown. My eyes chandeliers and them below, stuffing me back into myself.

The glass is wide. The sky will feast. They scatter, now, these painted beasts. I do not know where all the water goes.

And still they do not look. They do not look. They do not look.

The Art of Saving Other People

We never meant for her to give
birth inside a church. Pass the towels
you said, like you'd done this before.
The energy-saving light bulbs bouncing
off your hair gel.
We haven't got no towels, I said
looking around and seeing only paper stacks.
I considered swallowing them whole
to start a fire within myself.
Where are the people? you asked,
abandoned fishing rods by the holy font.
The three of us kneeling on
knitted prayer mats.
We fed her ice cream to remind us of childhood days.
Between the yells and shooting pains
I counted candles. Twelve, half-expecting
wings to come. For a bird to be birthed
on the cold stone floor.
To have to take her home to mother inside a cage.
For her to whistle.
For the blue glass lambs to carol-sing.
In the car, we'd guessed some names
by traffic lights – bemused that we
could walk upright compared to animals.
Our breath dragon smoke.
You could be a window, right now,
you said. Up there, high, in three bright colours.
Which colours? I said
seeing all of them in bloody orbs.
My hands, and yours, crushed chestnuts roasting.
Her stomach an ark-sized orange fruit.

Orange Brain. Flowered Brain.

Abigail's mind is aal ablaze. Gaspin.
    Her thumbnails twistin, jellyfish.
        At neet, swimmin yem, her bubbleface.
            How can w'breathe, like bulbous whales?

She wishes hard on lion rocks.
In sunlight, takes out her grapefruit brain.
Laughin, laughin, canny broad.   Fer she can hold hersel.

Crouchin down and drippin out.

Her brain, right, is an orange fruit.
A peel-back stone.   Girl segmented: pulsin. Caald.

She pictures growin bairns on hangin trees.
Like them'd burst right outta themselves someday.

Keel aawa or gan fly away.

Angel bairns. Flower bairns.   Animal – aalways – animal.

Underwater, them's museums there.
Ships and them with gobs just wide.
Abigail with her brain on string.   Grafflin. Aalways grafflin.

Wor Abigail cups her brain like soft-shell crab.
Thinks o'throwin it.   Ter watch it gan from gapin holes.

Ter swim down and filter water through.

Kite-words | Girl-glass.
Hadaway in ter human wells.

In town, them talk of banishment. Ain't much time
fer them what split themselves.

On trees – see posters o'her impish face.
They say she'll feed hersel ter the gulls one day.

Afeared, she did run wild through the yella fields.
Seeking out a beak ter feed.   A yem ter roost.

Abigail rests hersel on the breathin cliffs.
            Her scattered brain | candied balloons.
                    Her soul canny-like a tatty ship.
                            A drowned out, metallic bird.

III

Hello, Dark

Look, I said. *Look.*

When we grow up we're not supposed to have things like favourite colours because, apparently, there are more important things in life.

But what does the colour orange sound like?

The funny thing is that I'm reading this to you from a piece of paper.

The funny thing is that I quite like the dark.

> My dark.
> Choosable dark.
> See you later, dark.

No, no, that's enough now.

Let's be lighthouses, instead.

I ask Google what it's like, being blind. And it comes up with 'What is being blind mean?' And I think *that's not very good English.* And Google says 'How do blind people dream?' And then lots of people start arguing on the internet.

People paint their houses with ridiculous names.

> Mermaid net.
> Flamingo's Tear.
> Whispering Teal.
> Phantom Mist.
> Grandma's Sweater.

I don't want to paint my house with Grandma's Sweater.

> It's loud in here.

The shape of words is very important. Here are some of my favourite words:

        skeleton   circus   onomatopoeia.

Troglobites are creatures that live in the entirely dark parts of caves. One of those is called a *phantom cave snail.*

        My doctor blinks.   He hands me a leaflet.

Once I went to a restaurant where we ate in the dark. All the waiters were blind and we couldn't see what we were eating. Every so often there was a crash as plates toppled to the floor and we carried on, regardless. The food was nice. You thought you could hear people groping each other on the other side of the room.

        Sighted people left feeling smug and ridiculous.

                What colour is chaos?

Scientists still don't know what most of the universe is made of so, perhaps, it's ok if I just sit here and think for a while.

If I can't see myself then perhaps that means I can be everywhere and everything.

I have a feeling this is incorrect.
But let's go with it.
It sounds good.

        Hello, dark.

Please don't let me make a fool of myself.

                    My favourite colour is green.

Butterfly Dresses at the Westminster Aquarium (1880)

The fabrics at the Freak Show move with the eyes of the watching.
Mannequins posing by trees as underwater plants, spots on their
skirts with ladybirds growing.

Scientists place their bets at the smoke-filled bar. Jokes of 'legless'
coat the black-pointed tongues. Their shirts striped as bumblebees
losing their queen.

Rich women enter and walk the carpet as an auction house. A
photographer's wife snaps The Tripod Man, slapping her tea-
stained legs to see if his move.

The prints around their necks are modelled on the limbless so
they can hang like meat. The Bear Lady and The Skeleton Man
sip beer, pointing knitting needles to both their hearts.

All are cloaked in Midas fur. There will be no touching. Pregnant
women peer through the locks, clutching their stomachs for fear
their eyes will become plastic dolls.

For fear that this is all catching. Maternal impressions of Sunday
best Venus de Milos – and the waiters with their wooden crosses,
pausing at every face.

What the Bearded Lady Told Me

(after Katerina Brac)

That she's never been called girl.
That the word girl sounds like a type of tree to her.
That her mother grew trees in rows in the back garden.
That she liked to count them.
That sometimes she covers her face in paper.
That she hates bubblegum.
That she likes travelling if she doesn't know where she is going.
That one day she would like to go whale-watching.
That she takes photographs inside her own head.
That she likes to stretch her mouth wide.
That she gave up on her legs such a very long time ago.
That between her legs is volcanic.
That men are terrified.
That she loves how terrified they are.
That she likes the sea.
That there's a bus that goes past her house the colour of fists.
That she grows into shapes when no one else is watching.

I Heard She Had a Strawberry Heart

She came up encased in deepest mud. She came, then, to stand up in a field. Planted herself. Her heart pulled to the highest branch. Its green strawberry pulse. A fruit-covered sarcophagus. Pips pushing out from the inside. From the other side.   From another place.

The villagers came. They stood and gaped. Heralding lists of Apostles she might answer to. They prayed for monsoons to wash her clean. They licked their lips, picked her heart string. One pilgrim wrote: *it would take a giant's hand to reach*. They nodded, then swayed, witnessing her religion.

Their wives had timers in their kitchen drawers. Egg belts across their ageing stomachs. Their view the red glow of a farmer's crop. Their husbands there with their brand new spades. Suspicion etched on every face.

For this strange girl – decked in bloom.

The Glow-worm Chasers

We ride to school in green barrows
our balloon heads   forever growing.

In the forest we unstitch ourselves.

Bow to one another in the shadows
of syrup trees.

We have one hour to decide which one of us is mortal.

We are light bulbs.

We give gifts of Christingles to light up the leaves.

Kitchen

What would you do if I died right now, here, you asked.
Your hand still resting on my thigh. Your eyes focused on the ceiling –
on the splash of curry sauce to the left of the light which doesn't work.

We could have been in a field.
A wooden spoon dug into my back.
I thought it funny.
Let's not talk of death where food is prepared, I said.

You turned away, stood up and opened the fridge.
The light shone past you. An outline of you

your feet tapping on the floor. Your mother would be home soon.
To her yellow and white check tea towels and her hand-painted bread bin

and her naked daughter standing like Jesus
in front of the refrigerator. I grabbed your foot.
Come on, your nipples'll freeze and you'll be cryogenically frozen.
There was a laugh somewhere, under your hair, as you toppled backwards
onto the floor and cupped my face.
So if I died, right here, now, you said – you'd freeze me?
Your eyes were grey, round. You were swimming
and I didn't know what you wanted me to do.

I'd keep you, I said. I'd keep you right here.
Dead? You grinned. Where food is prepared?
Well then I'd eat you, I said, and you stared so deep I drowned
in a kitchen that wasn't there.

I'd swallow down all the evidence of you.

I grabbed your hand.
We heard a key turn in a front door, somewhere by the shore.
I'd like that, you said, and then kissed me.

How to Weigh Nothing

We drive until there are no more mirrors.
Straight up the A1, wet flip-flops on the peddle
before our ride flanks oak trees. Your kid sister in the back
trying to put mascara on straight. When nights fall
we pull into fields that are yet to have names.
You lock the doors from the inside so our skeletons
can shine and not be disturbed. In the mornings we begin again.
Go past a choir on the motorway huddled
near a hot dog stand. Truckers watch them. You wind
the window to the bottom so they swallow down Bowie.
The three of us spend the next mile with burnt onions giggling
on the base of our tongues. Like popping candy. Suddenly we're in
a whole new country. I find a book in the glove box to learn
the language of the road signs. Shape my gums into diphthongs
that disappear down my blouse. You count new five pound notes
when we pull up for petrol. They rustle like mum's keys.
I pretend this is an adventure. We calm ourselves down.

In Fields She Wasn't Scarin Crows

In corn, the girls mine down fer words. *Petty. Gannin. Bird-face. Coppa.*
Sweat tricklin awaa their mud-stained ayes.   This were the way of it.

Piecemeal recklessness – the sea awash w'greyin yarns. Their red meat
ears, their telephones. Buzzin down inside themselves. Their savin graces.

Faces buried from them runnin yem. Lads watchin lasses out t'scare the
crows. Fer under dresses she's been runnin aal and aalways aawa

forest floors. Bare foot, rabbit breath, and dished up hearts. Back yem
is bears, back yem is words she cannot cage. Mining fer *mine*, fer *wor*

fer under aal their dirt, the earth beats hard inside her chest.
                                                    There she gans.
She, the miner bird. Singin out her blackened voice – shoutin out fer words.

On Display at the Hunterian Museum

Hold w'bodies to the light
                and fire us up with electricity.
      See w'saintly
catchin graces with w'netted skin and bone.

Call w'home with all the names
what were stammered throughout history
                what were caged around w'memories,
what were pummelled and were sewn.

The Woman's Private Looking-glass

Take the physician's advice.

Forget imagination and do not look straight at the moon.
Up there devil-girls cradle silver eggs. They slide
from roller coaster innards, trickle tales
of the greats.

> *Leda, Lilith, Sirin* – all owl-chested women.

And do not peer into the sea; for there salted-tadpoles twist around
your organs and turn your baby into stone. It is well known that
climbing mountains breeds giants, forest-beards and babes tossed
into the woods. And it is understood that touching an animal seeps
under your skin until every wild child resembles lions and lynx.
What do they think of pulling concertina bairns out of red-raw
wombs? Inner rooms reserved for the most complicated monsters.

Let the gossips build the cage, dragged to our city's centre stage.
Let the world come. Let it pay a grand sum to gawp at
all our animal children.

> The Tiger-Striped Lass.　　　The Dog-faced Lad.
>
> The Hairy Maid at the Harpsichord.
>
> The Horned Girl.　　　The Swedish Giant.
>
> The Lobster Boy.　　　The Lobster Girl.
>
> The Pig-Faced Lady of Manchester Square.
>
> The Man of the Woods.　　　The Victorian Mummy.

And isn't it funny how, now, we morph our fingers into keys.

    Magpied. Glittering.
    Picking locks to skitter   out of all our silver boxes.

Whether we are more or less bodied than the rule book states,
I anticipate us diving into uncharted lakes.

    Babes, there's no going back now.

Smash this circus to the ground.   Howl fiercely at the moon.

The Day We Ran Away from the Circus

I

The sky fell
we fell into the sky
the sun was.
We were.

II

We took our photographs
and stuck them
cloudwards.

The tide engorged then
                    and all was green.

III

In this new world, there are forests and duck-feet shoes.

There is us, there.

      Waiting.

      Our crow mouths full of feathers.

We are stamping.
Stamping. Stamping.

            Stamping our newborn feet.

Jen Campbell grew up by the sea. She is a bestselling author and award-winning poet. Her most recent books include a short story collection, *The Beginning of the World in the Middle of the Night*, and a series of children's picture books about a book-loving dragon called Franklin. She won the Jane Martin Poetry Prize in 2013, received an Eric Gregory Award in 2016, is Vlogger in Residence for the Poetry Book Society, and was a judge of the Forward Prize in 2018. She talks about books, fairy tales and disfigurement at youtube.com/jenvcampbell. Her poetry pamphlet *The Hungry Ghost Festival* was published by *The Rialto* in 2012, and her first book-length collection, *The Girl Aquarium*, by Bloodaxe Books in 2019. She lives in London.

www.ingramcontent.com/pod-product-compliance
Lightning Source LLC
Jackson TN
JSHW080855211224
75817JS00002B/57